14 angels

THE SEVEN HOLY VIRTUES AND THE SEVEN DEADLY SINS

SECOND EDITION

TEXT, ART AND DESIGN BY JCHOOPER

14 Angels © 2021 jchooper. All rights reserved.
No part of this book may be reproduced in any form without written permission of the author.

CHARITY	4
CHARITY	4
HOPE	6
HOPE	6
COURAGE	8
COURAGE	8
TEMPERANCE	10
TEMPERANCE	10
FAITH	12
FAITH	12
JUSTICE	14
JUSTICE	14
WISDOM	16
WISDOM	16
LUST	18
LUST	18
AVARICE	20
AVARICE	20
GLUTTONY	22
GLUTTONY	22
SLOTH	24
SLOTH	24
ENVY	26
ENVY	26
ANGER	28
ANGER	28
PRIDE	30
PRIDE	30

introduction

Virtue is positive behavior, strength. Virtues are the foundation of morality, good, individual greatness. Sin is an offensive fault, a weakness. It is an act that violates moral rule; a regrettable transgression.

Years ago, I read a study about the seven deadly sins, a concept that dates back to early Christianity, which led me to the question of which one of these sins was pointing at me. Being that none of us are absolutely good or absolutely evil, I started to research the virtues as well. This study pushed me into beautiful and scary places within my soul, feeding on joy, shame and many memories of past experiences. During this research I was exposed to the work of many artists who have created visual interpretations of these concepts. I though some of them were missing the mark, so I decided to create my own set. I was directed to delve into a deep study of each one of them and quickly learned the difficulty of my quest; to depict a spirit/passion in a visual form.

My findings inspired me to represent them as angels; being that they often appear in human form. I believe the human figure is one of the most beautiful things in creation, and it is certainly the vehicle through which our souls experience these virtues and sins. While I approach these subjects from my own Christian perspective, I understand that the viewer will experience them through the veil of their own culture and religious upbringing. Therefore, I tried to stay away from specifics and adopt a more universal tone, while avoiding being too obvious or simple. Each description includes some references for your personal study.

One of the things I learned on this journey is that ignorance of self often leads to sin, to unhappiness and self-destruction. I hope the reader can look inward, as well as outward, to delight and marvel in this wonderful experience that is life, and in the process, find encouragement, inspiration and their own truth.

charity

Charity is voluntary help; it is meeting the needs of others. Anyone who has experienced charity has experienced love.

Charity is Christian love, an unlimited kindness towards others. Love is practical and real. It is giving without expecting anything in return. God does not need us; he loves us. God has given His only Son for our salvation because we need Him; therefore, love is a huge part of salvation. In turn, Jesus has taught us to love one another. Those who love the Father, Son and Holy Spirit follow His commandments.

READ 1 CORINTHIANS 13:4-7 & JOHN 3:16

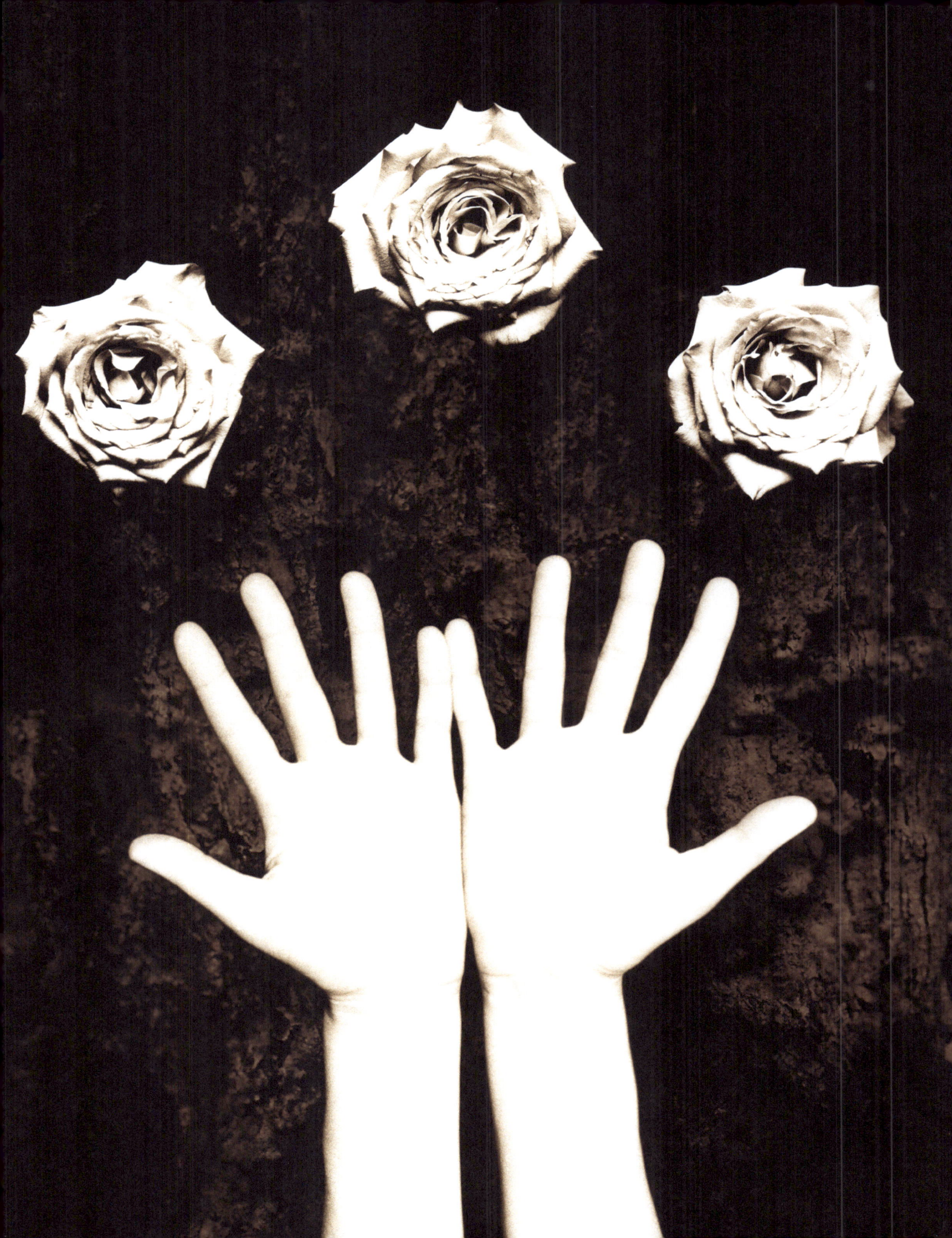

hope

Hope is the belief in a positive outcome. It is trust and its time frame is the future. Wisdom, faith and past experiences can be sources of hope. A natural consequence of hope is peace of mind.

Our relationship with the Father should be one of hope. We hope that God will look after us, just like a mother or father looks after her or his own offspring, protecting them and making sure all their needs are met. We should not expect to get all that we ask for, just like a child makes unwise requests, but to receive exactly what we need. Our understanding is limited, so we need to trust His wisdom. Our relationship with God is built on a strong covenant, one that is not easily broken, because the Holy Father is not willing to give it up.

READ DEUTERONOMY 31:8 & PROVERBS 3:5-6

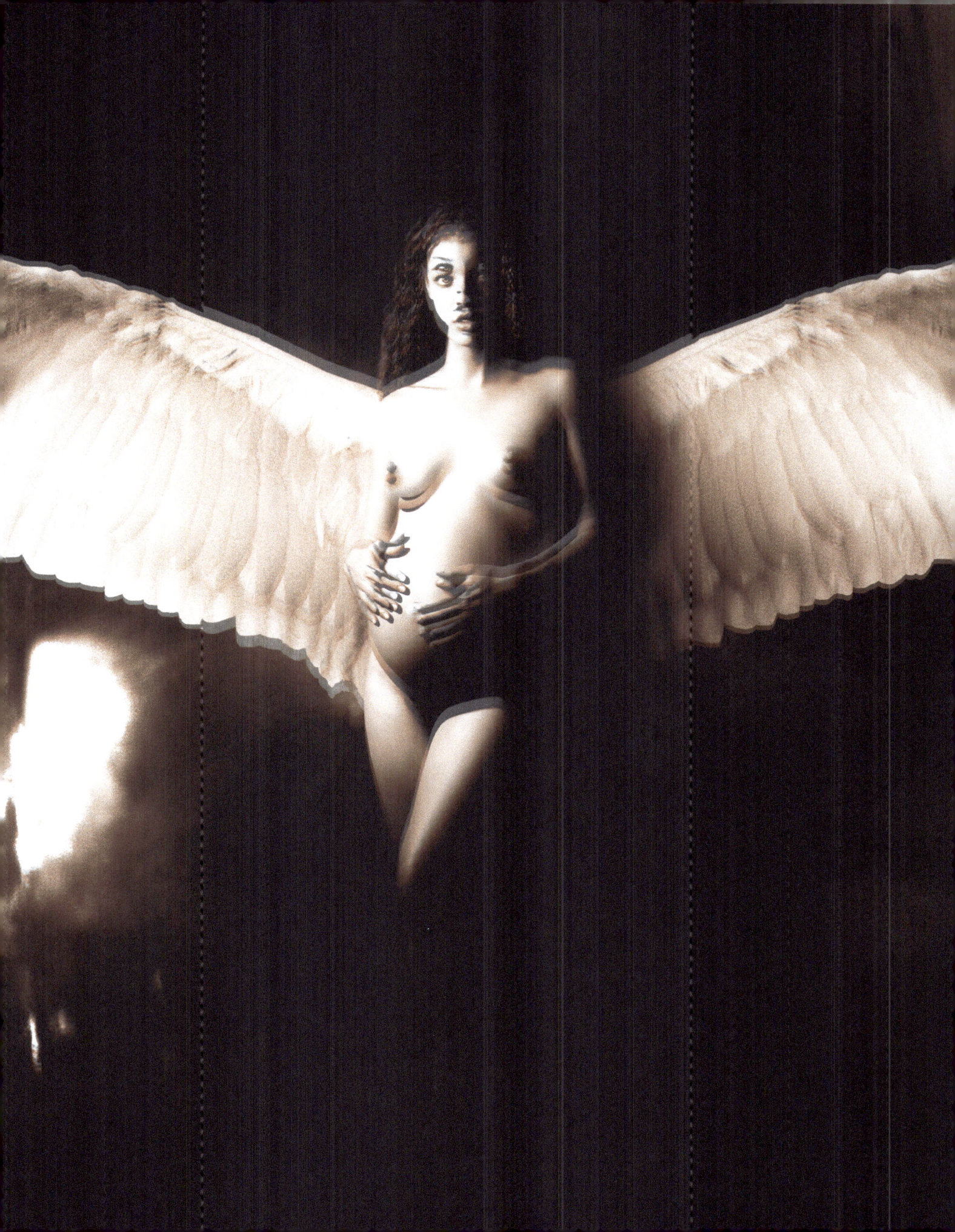

courage

Courage is the ability to do something frightening; it is venturing, persevering, and withstanding danger, fear, or difficulty. Courage is also the possession of moral or physical strength in the face of pain or grief.

We are constantly tested by life, either when we face personal danger or when we face our responsibilities. Courage is knowing what is right based on the law, wisdom, and past experience, and goes beyond common sense. Courage gives us the inner strength to make tough choices. God does not ask us to take the easy way, but to carry our own cross and follow Him. We have to die to our ways and be reborn in His ways. Courage is not blind, and we are instructed to face challenges without fear and equipped with the power of his might.

READ DEUTERONOMY 31:6 & EPHESIANS 6:10-18

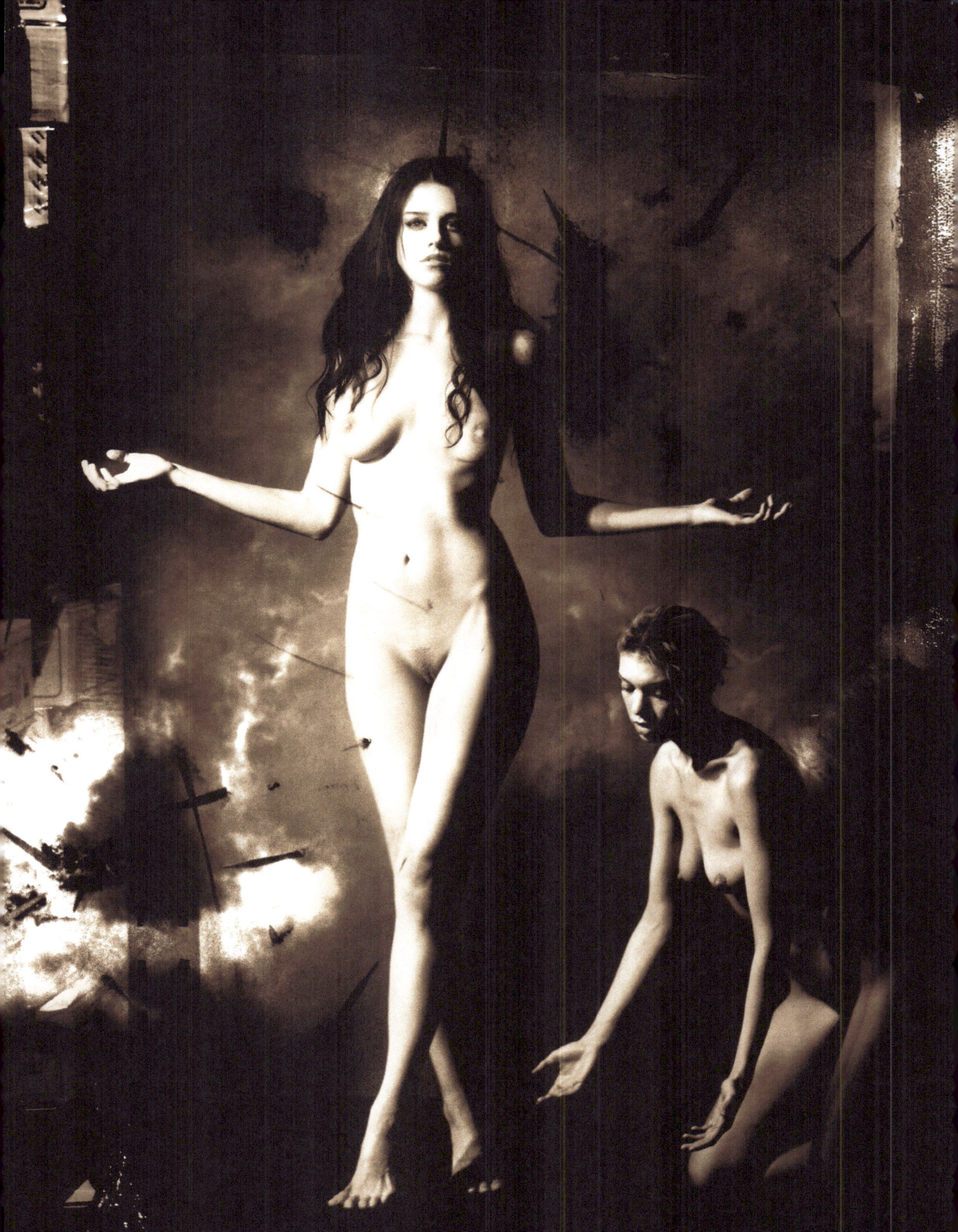

temperance

Temperance is strength of character and is the foundation for other positive qualities such as abstinence, chastity, modesty, humility, prudence, self-control, moderation, forgiveness, and mercy. It is restraint from impulsive behavior, such as sexual desire, vanity, greed, or anger.

Temperance is a doorway to communication, a stronghold, a bridge that leads to victory. It is a teacher that leads by example. Jesus was able to bring the dead back to life, to heal the sick, give sight to the blind, and to subdue demons. Jesus was tempted in many ways yet didn't opt for that. He didn't elect to defend himself against his accusers nor to summon legions of angels to stop his crucifixion, He decided to fulfill the scriptures for our sake. That form of restraint is a perfect example of temperance.

READ COLOSSIANS 3:12 & 1 PETER 3:15

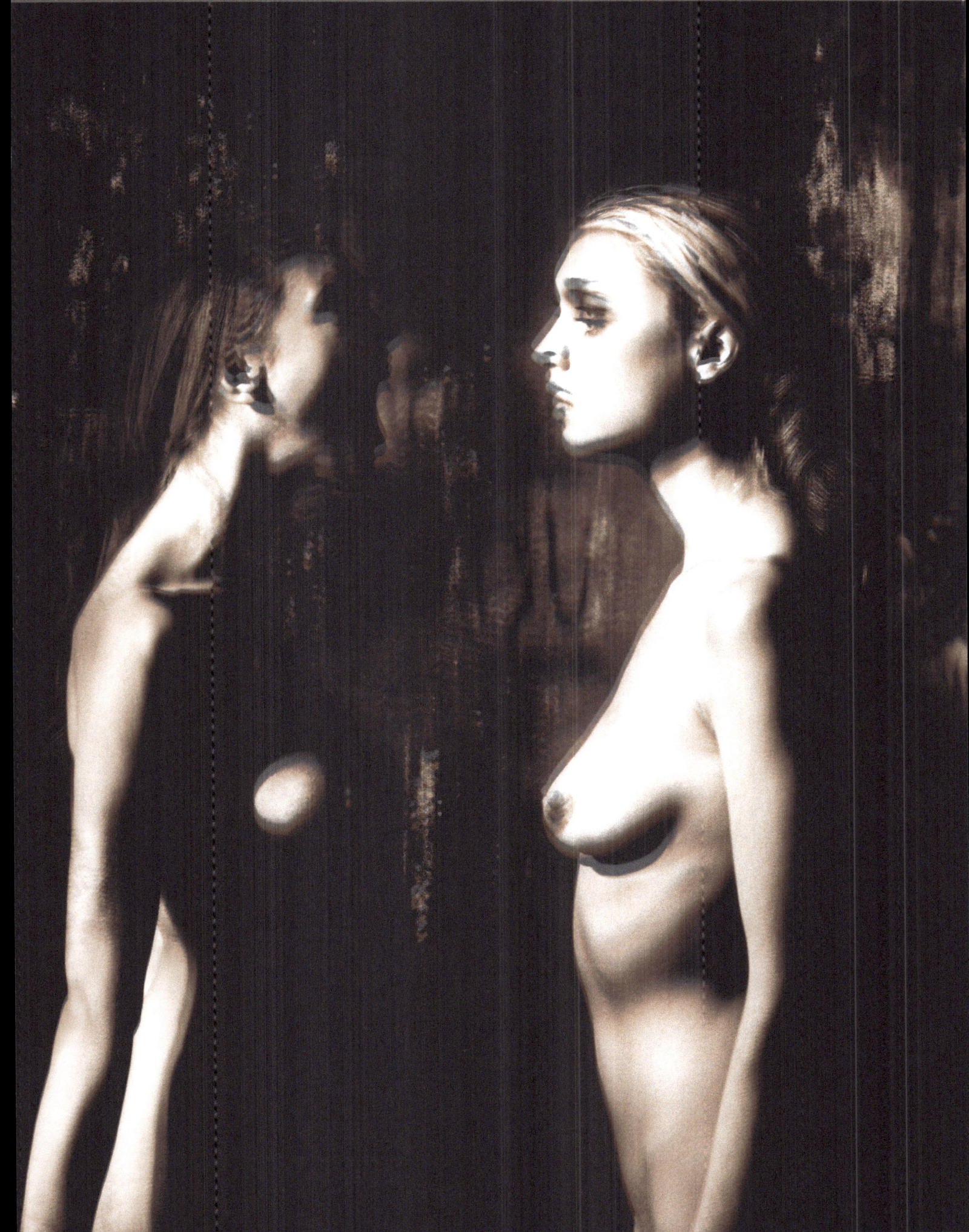

faith

Faith is complete trust and settles questions that sometimes cannot be resolved by evidence, often in opposition with reason. Faith is the evidence of things not seen. Faith's time frame is the present, based on belief. It is sometimes confused with hope. Hope is wishing something to be true in the future, an outcome, but faith is knowing something to be true now. Faith is the assurance of things hoped for, and that is why it is an absolute requirement for answered prayer.

The belief in God, His doctrines, teachings, and promises comes through faith. It comes from the heart and not merely from reason, which means it can be experienced without physical proof. Faith is the belief in miracles, in a spiritual world, in things that cannot be seen nor understood. Faith provides inner strength, and it is grounded in the Word of God.

READ ROMANS 10:17 & COLOSSIANS 2:5

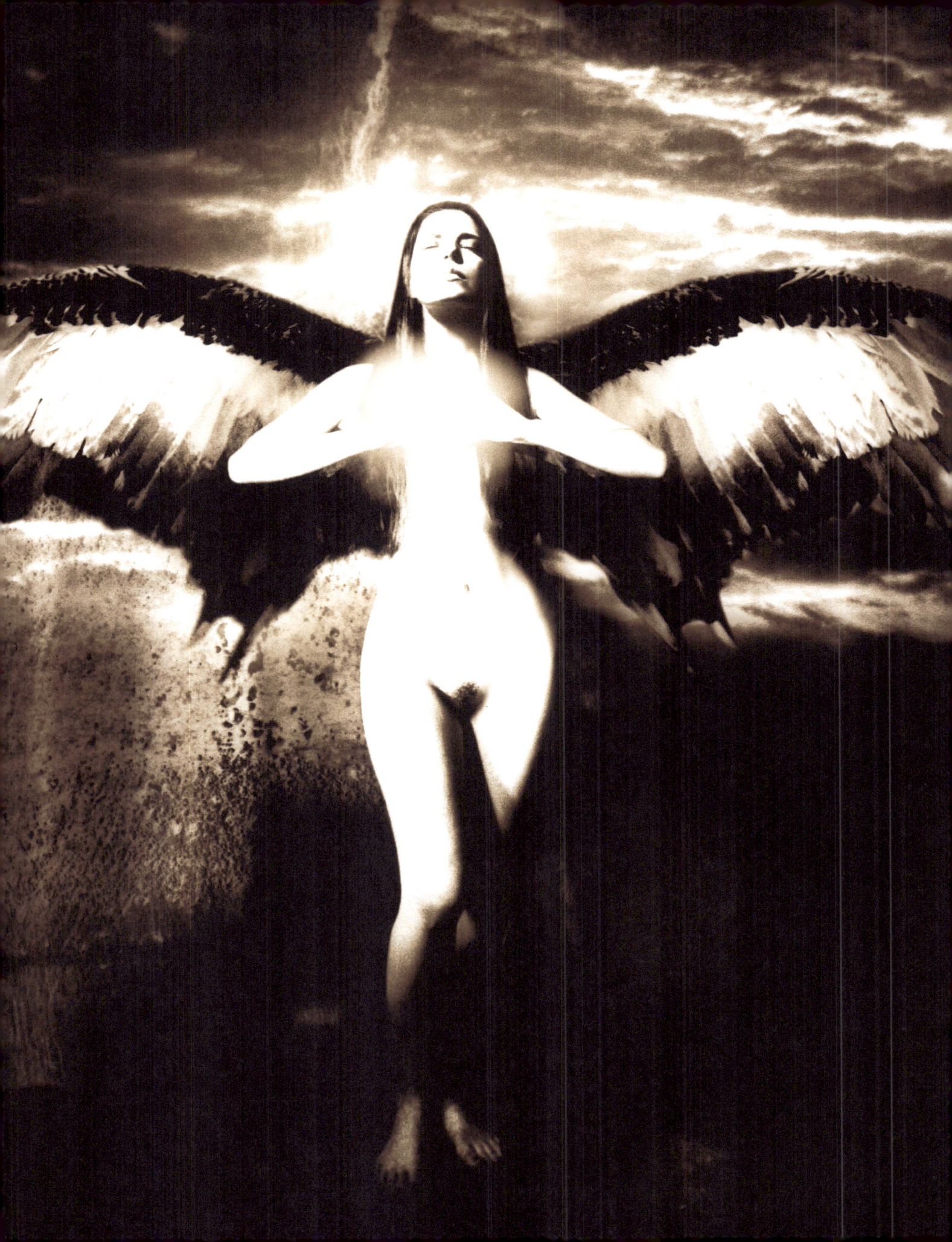

justice

Justice is a harmonious relationship, truth; it is to receive the exact equivalent of what has been given. In order for justice to be served, freedom of choice must be present. The level to which the offender is aware of the consequences of his/her action may be the determining factor in his judgment and retribution.

The intention of justice is to make the victim whole and to reintegrate the offender. Jesus, being both man and God, is the ultimate judge. When we sin, we commit an offense against God and are subject to His judgment. The Bible tells us that Jesus has paid for our sins, and no retribution is demanded. It is only through our belief in His Word and our acceptance of his sacrifice that we are spared from judgment; therefore, redemption takes place based on faith.

READ MATTHEW 7:1-5 & JOHN 5:24-29

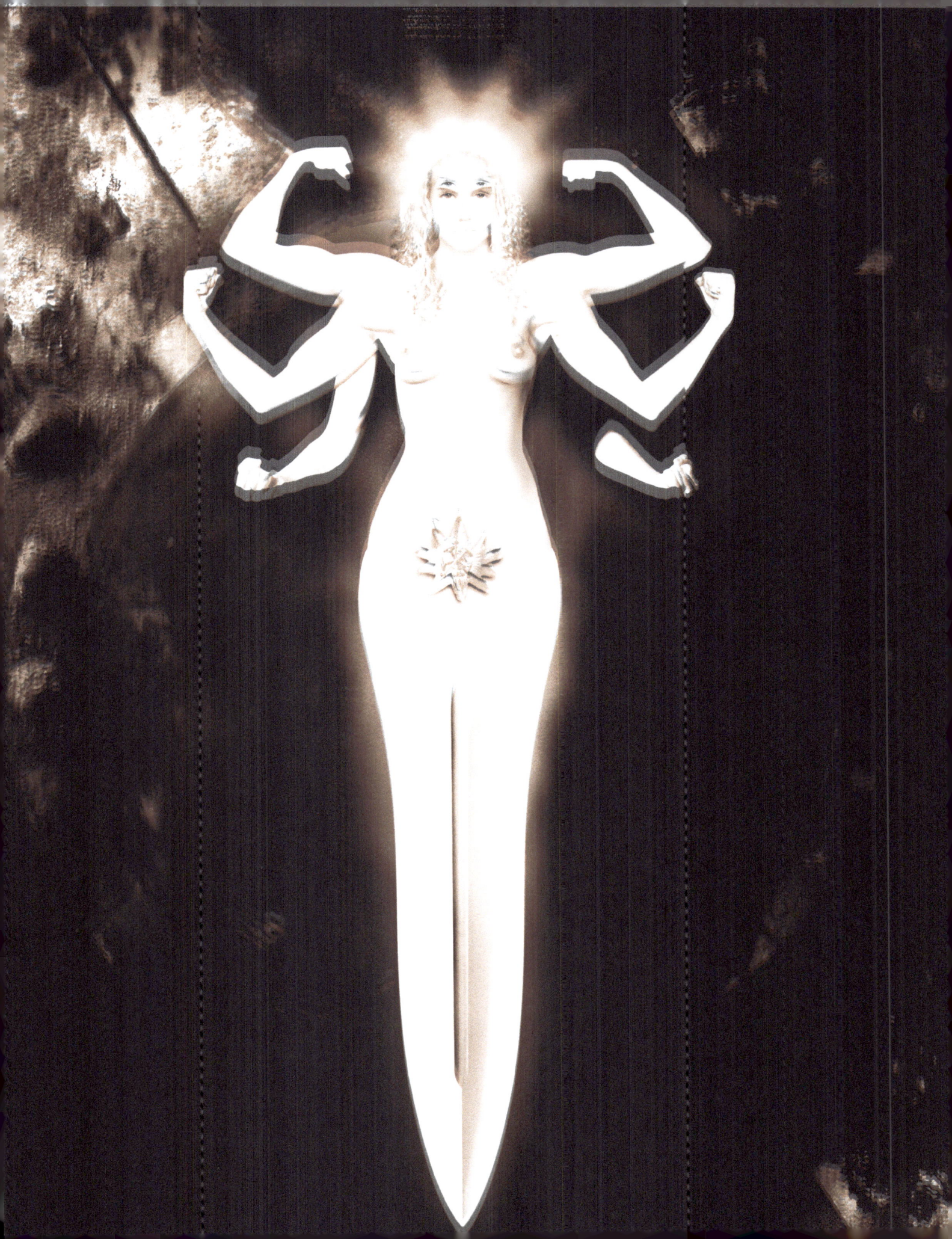

Wisdom

Wisdom is considered the source of all virtues, the capacity to act righteously with good judgment and understanding. Wisdom is the virtue of having knowledge and experience. Some refer to it as common sense or practical knowledge.

There is both secular and divine wisdom, and the latter is much more valuable. A common way of acquiring wisdom is through adversity. It is through challenges that people learn and grow in spirit. Wisdom is cumulative; it comes with age and truth, through life. Following this principle, God has a level of wisdom that cannot be surpassed. Through wisdom comes fear of the Lord, and therefore it is a powerful ally against sin.

READ JOB 28:28 & PROVERBS 2:6

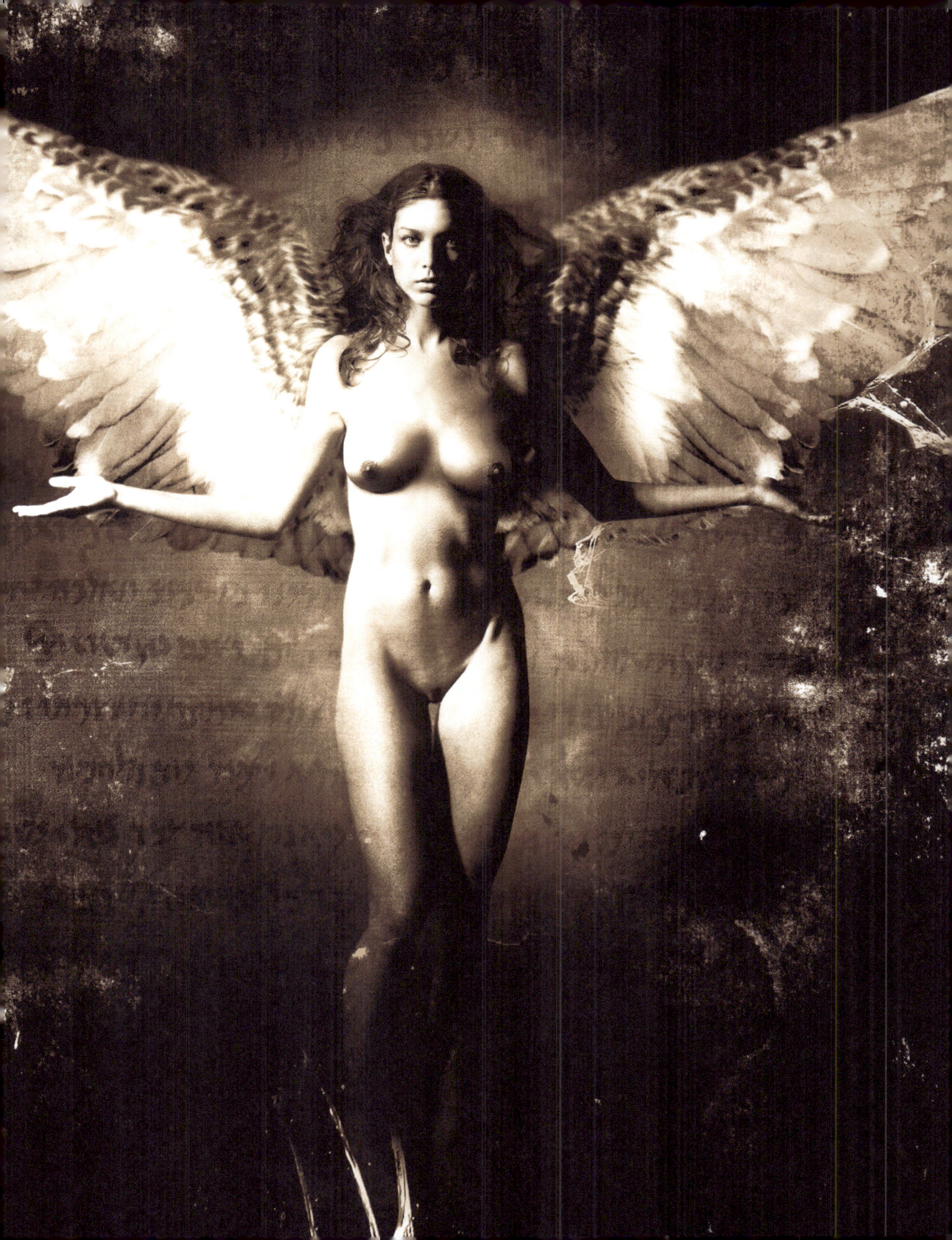

lust

Lust is the uncontrolled desire for a person, object or experience. It is a lack of control over passions and wants. Lust is an excessive obsession that leads to pain, suffering and eventual isolation. An excessive desire for sex, power, fame, or other indulgence can turn addictive and control the individual, transformed into an endless pursuit that eventually becomes the reason for someone's existence: an idol.

Lust is usually associated with sex. Sex is part of God's design for humankind and part of life, and must have its place in our lives, Sex should not be totally repressed and ignored, but an expression of love. Lust is not connected with love; it is selfish, an insatiable hunger. We are called to have temperance and wisdom; to love others as ourselves.

READ ROMANS 1:24-28 & MATTHEW 22:37-39

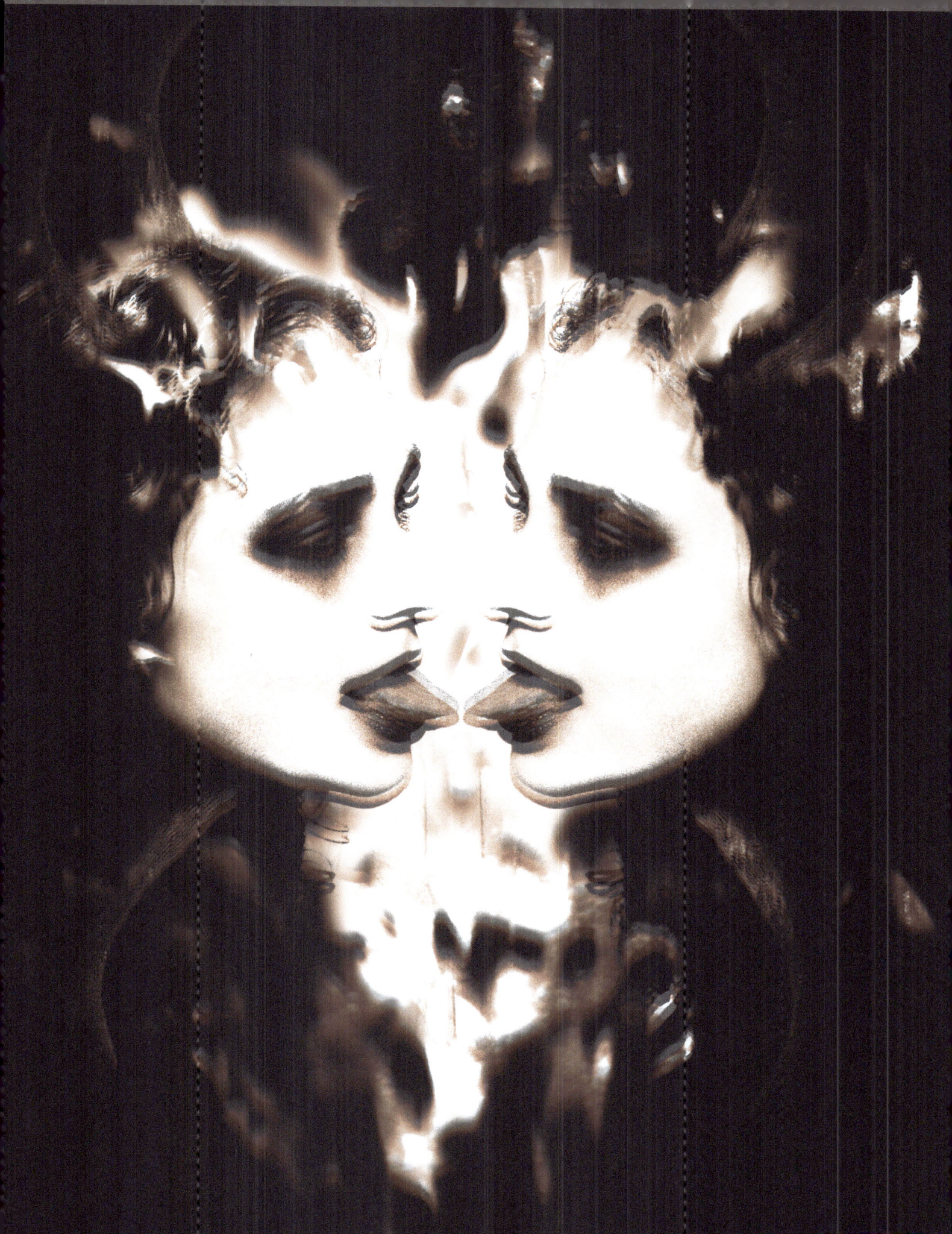

avarice

Avarice is extreme greed for wealth and earthly possessions; the desire and pursuit to hoard things, to possess far beyond what is needed. Avarice is a sin of excess that can lead to bribery, disloyalty, betrayal, violence, deceit, and loneliness.

Money by itself is neither good nor bad, it is simply a resource, and it can be very difficult to live with or without, depending on the situation. A person suffering from avarice usually feels the need to be totally independent from others, to be in full control of their destiny and wealth, regardless of measure, how it was obtained, or if others are suffering due to this selfish endeavor. While it is true massive accumulation of material possessions can provide a sense of security, it also makes the person a target. Therein lies the big deception, money turns their masters into their servants, and becomes their idol.

READ 1 CORINTHIANS 6:10 & MATTHEW 6:24 & 19:24

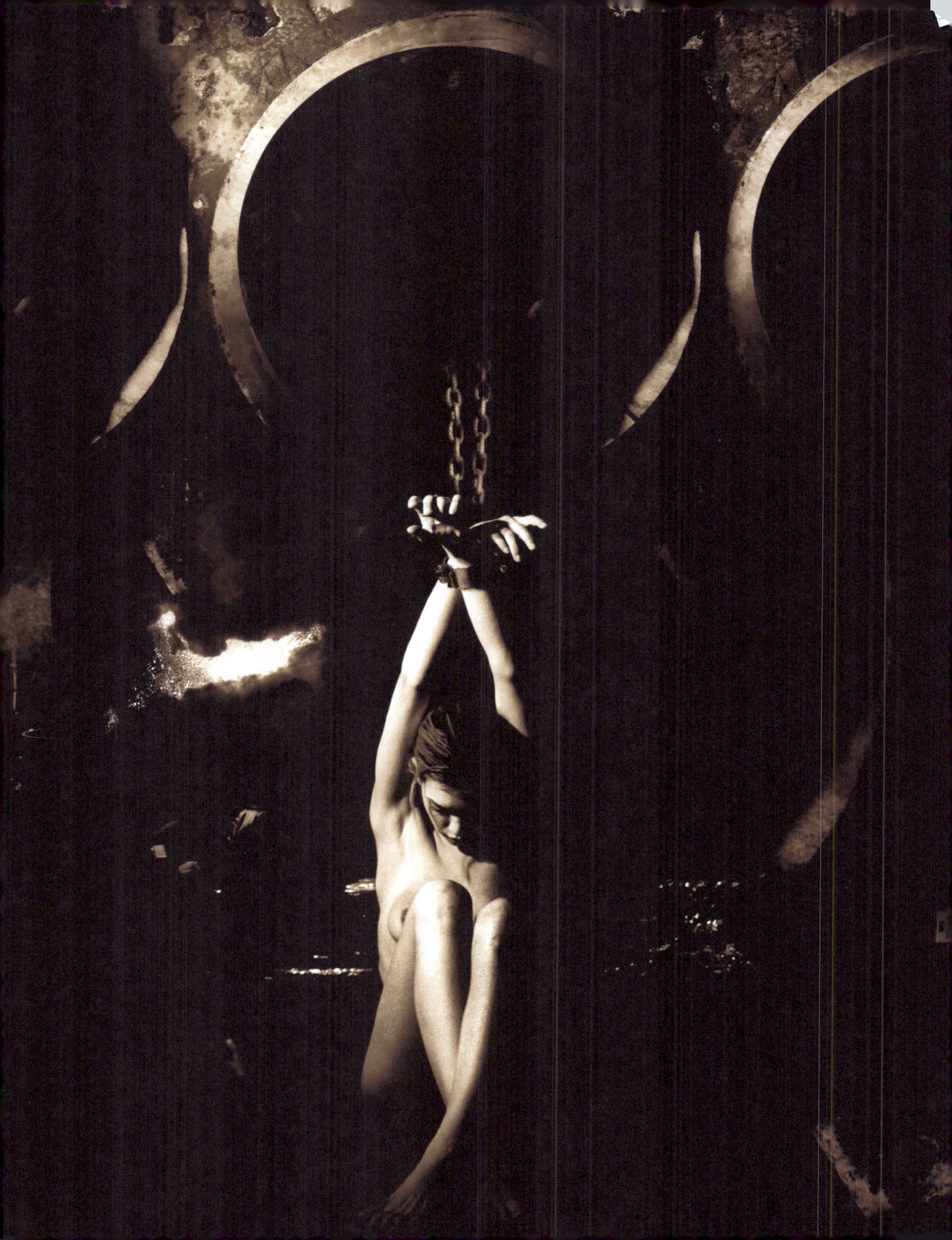

gluttony

Gluttony means to ingest in over-indulgence. It is over-consumption of food, drink, or substances to the point where it becomes a progressive and self-destructive habit. Drug addictions, obesity, alcoholism — all are forms of gluttony.

Gluttony often is a reflection of spiritual pain. One may succumb to gluttony through hopelessness, stress, adversity, desperation or boredom. The first step for recovery is to heal those emotional wounds. The glutton must let go of pride and self-sufficiency and recognize the fact that those substances are unfit fillers for a void that can only be restored by a personal relationship with God. Once the love of self is restored, it is followed by the love of others. The awareness of God's love for each one of us, as we are in the present time, with all our flaws, is key to fight this form of self-hatred.

READ EZEKIEL 16:49 & PROVERBS 23:20-21

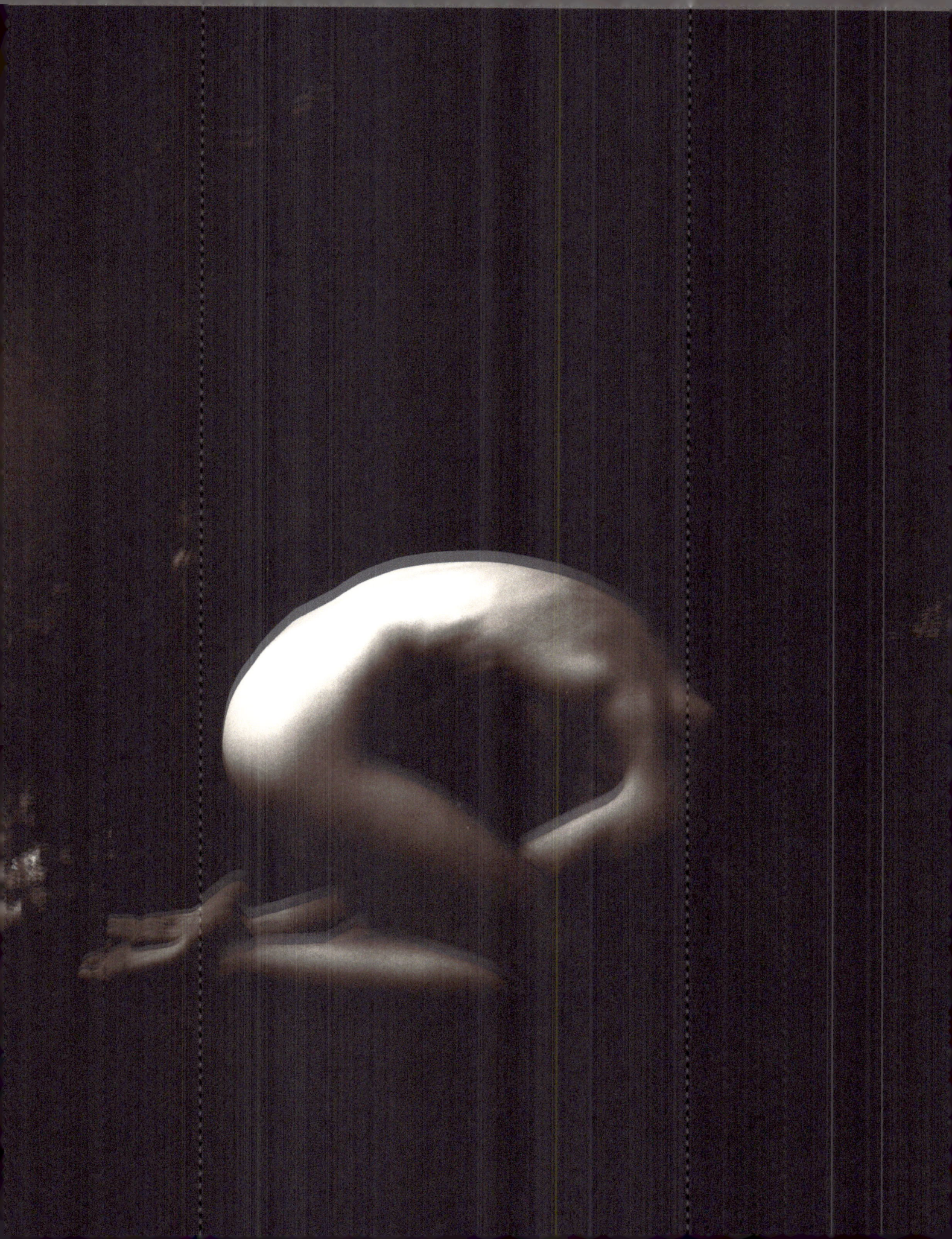

sloth

Sloth is despair, spiritual or emotional apathy that can be perceived as laziness or depression. Once it settles, it leads to being physically and emotionally inactive. It is the reluctance to make an effort, and ever-growing pit of despair and darkness.

Sloth is a separation from God; it is the opposite of hope. Evil prevails when good fails to act, and it is through a lack of purpose that sloth invites the desire to sin. Sloth leads to isolation and poverty, to the limitation of the human experience. When a person becomes inactive, his/her support becomes a burden to others and creates isolation. The person who falls into depression loses interest in society, and in turn, will be abandoned by it. Life is movement and a balanced lifestyle, a good measure of work and play, and a healthy body with a healthy mind. Positive prayer and thinking can bring enough light to show a path out of the despair. As long as there is life, there is hope. Never give up.

READ MATTHEW 25:30 & 2 PETER 1:5-9

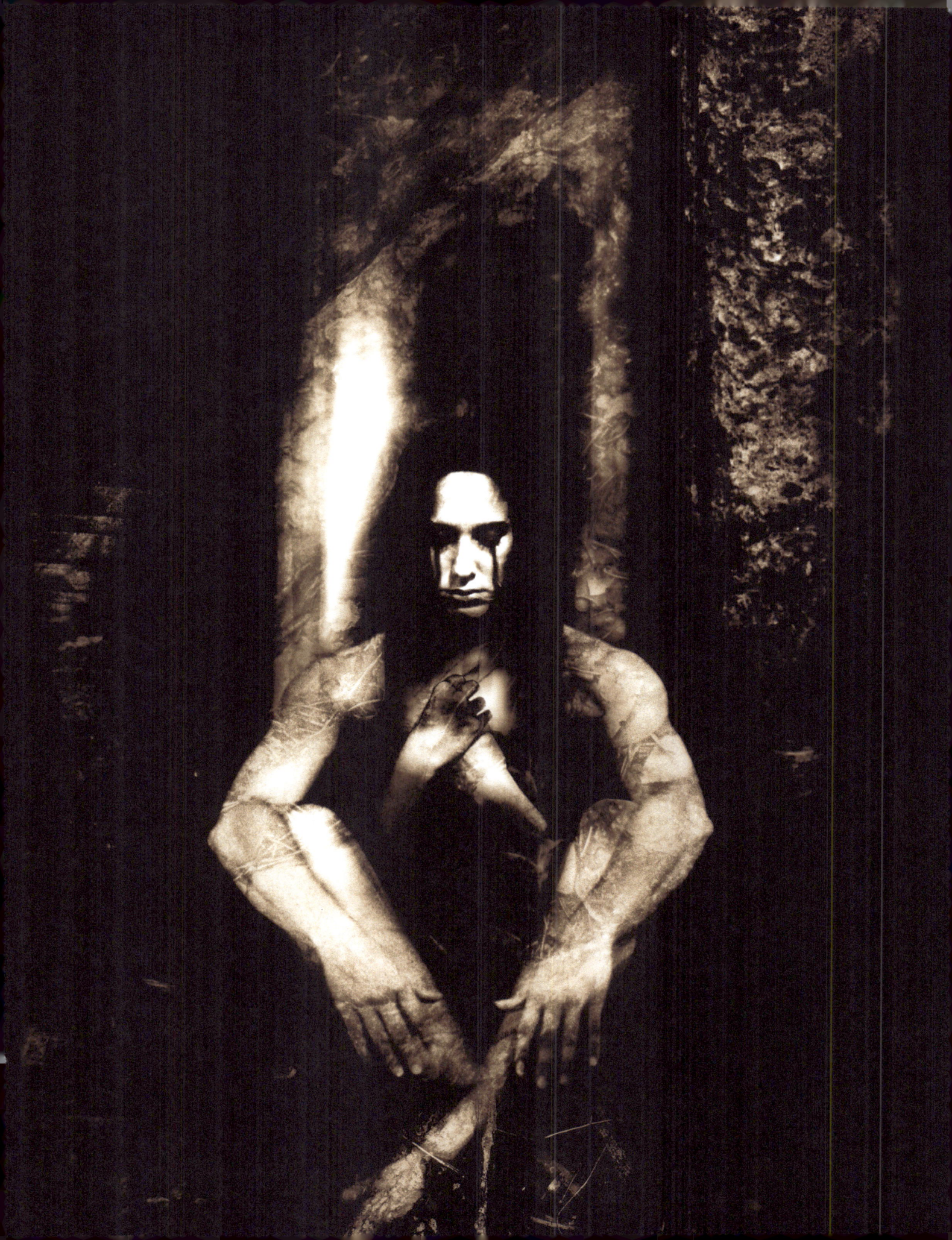

ENVY

Envy is a feeling of discontentment by means of comparison. It is the desire to acquire material things or qualities belonging to another, or to deny a person of those achievements.

Society tells us to be taller, stronger, faster, that we need to be materially successful. False expectations, deceptive dreams, and peer pressure can make us forget that the world, by design, is not fair. Envy is considered a motivational force by some, but its true nature comes to light when those goals cannot be achieved. Frustration sinks in and the gateway to sin is opened. Envy can make us incredibly unhappy. In addition, the idea to make others share our misery results in personal isolation and guilt. We need to learn to love ourselves and to accept the fact that we were created as individuals, with our own gifts and shortcomings. We were never meant to be perfect; we were meant to be unique.

READ ECCLESIASTES 4:4 & PROVERBS 23:17

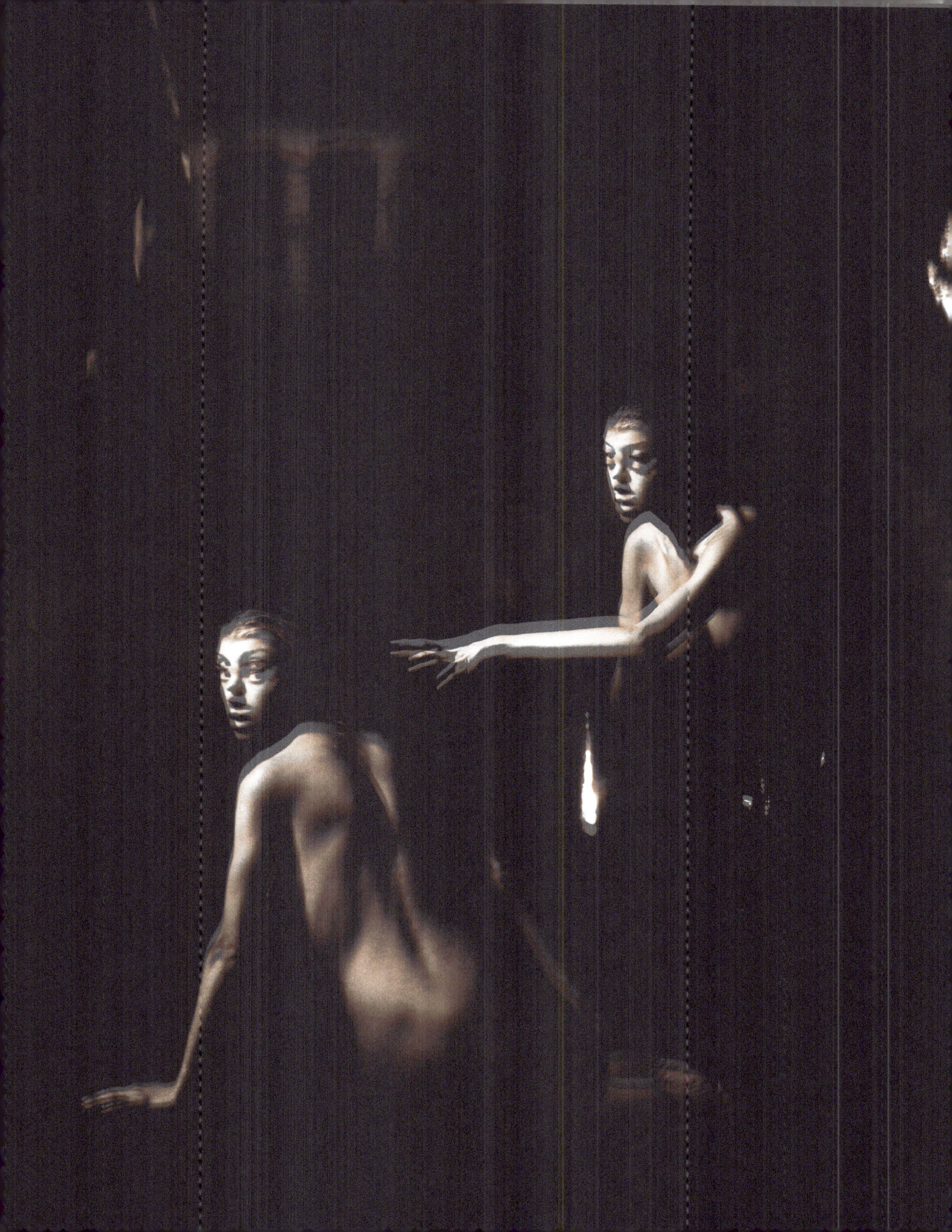

anger

Anger is a strong feeling of hate. It is exemplified by acts of hostility aroused by a perceived wrong and revenge-seeking. It is propelled by self-justification. Anger is probably the most visible sin and is often confused with violence. Violence by itself is not sinful; it is a natural behavior tied directly to survival, and a measure of anger is necessary for self-preservation.

Anger needs an expression, and repressed anger becomes a poison that either turns inwardly, resulting in a state of frozen depression, or outwardly, turning into bitterness, resentment, hate, and violence. Extreme anger is known as wrath. One of the worst aspects of anger is it may persist long after revenge has taken place, holding us captive and resulting in self-destruction. To prevent it a choice must be made: to let go of the offense. We need to forgive everyone, including ourselves.

READ PSALM 37:8 & COLOSSIANS 3:13

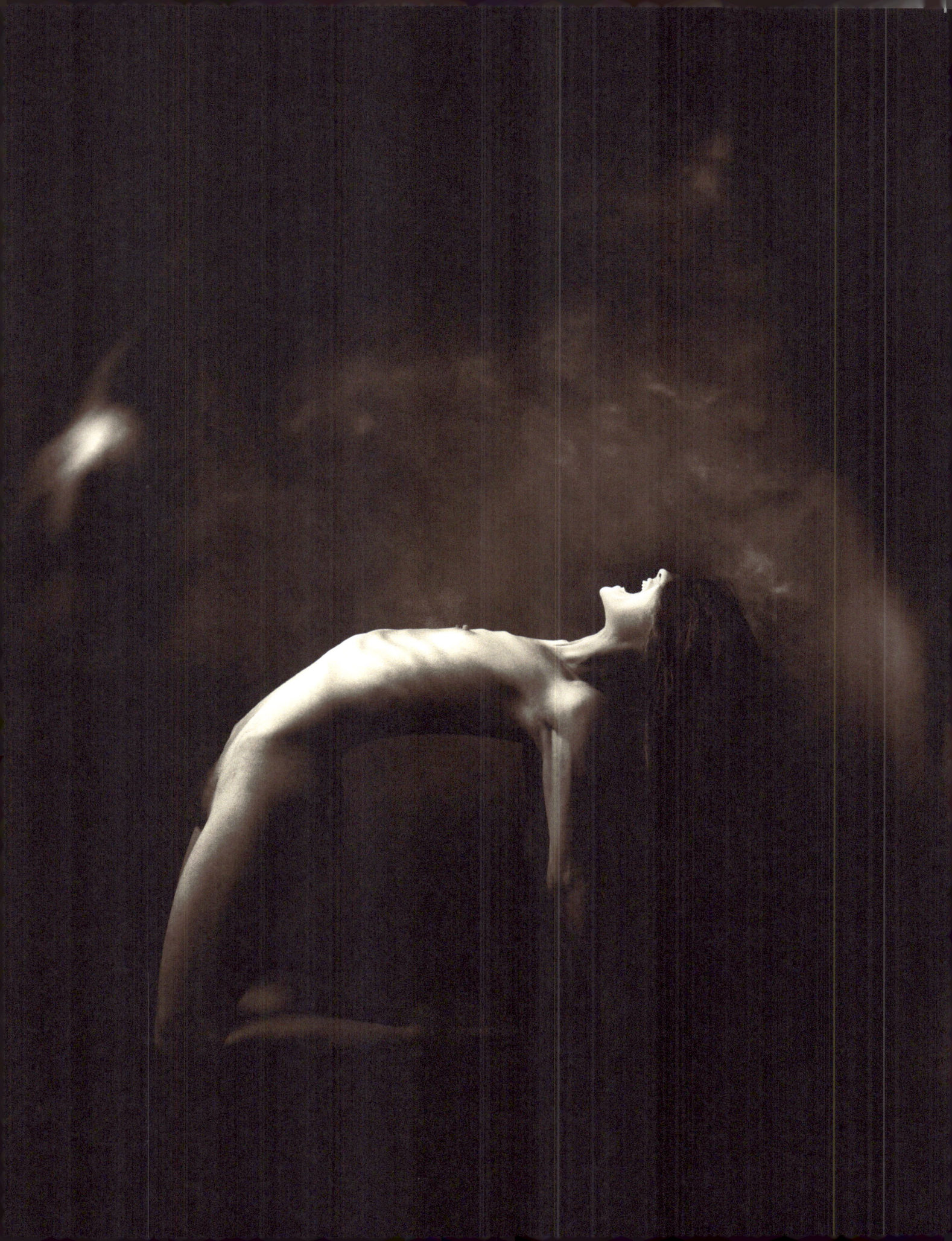

pride

Pride is inordinate self-esteem, arrogance arising from one's own achievements or merits. It is the excessive love of self, through which superiority is established regardless of the truth. Race, social class, financial status, power and other stereotypes teach us to repudiate others, so we feel superior to them.

A beautiful angel, the fallen one, the enemy of man, exalted himself above all, and is also called the father of pride. That is the sin that cost him to be cast out of heaven. Pride is considered the source of all the other sins. It leads to damnation and destruction, because it fails to acknowledge the good of others. This sin differs diametrically from the teachings and life of Jesus. He taught us to serve one another, and to be humble. It is only through the realization that we are ignorant that we can begin to understand others and accept our humble nature and design.

READ PSALM 10:4 & PHILIPPIANS 2:3-11

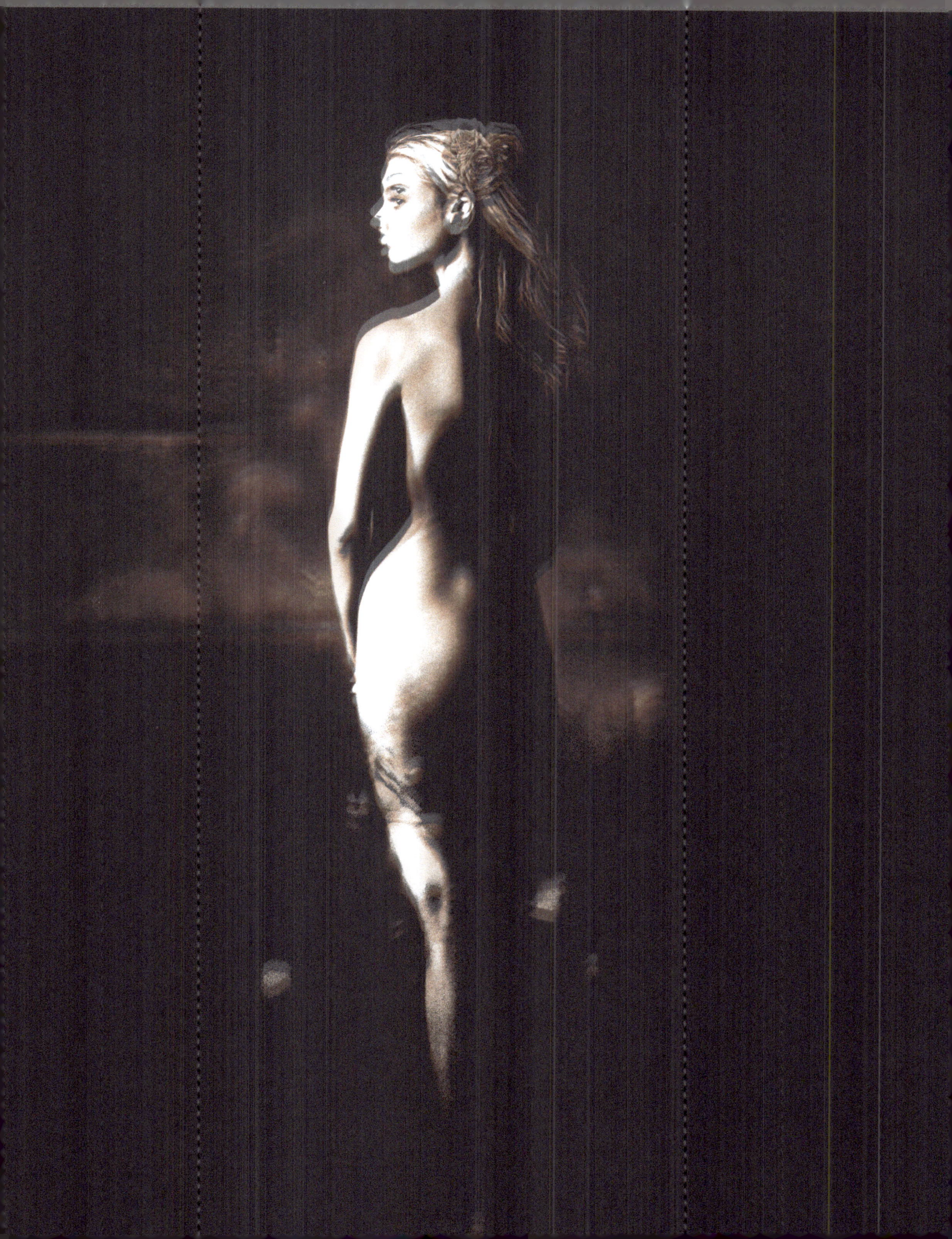

TRUTH WILL MAKE YOU FREE